MW00365879

WHISPERS IN MY DEEPEST NIGHTMARES

With love,
Allison

ALLISON HAILEY

authorHOUSE®

AuthorHouse™
1663 Liberty Drive
Bloomington, IN 47403
www.authorhouse.com
Phone: 833-262-8899

Published by AuthorHouse 11/03/2020

ISBN: 978-1-6655-0676-2 (sc)
ISBN: 978-1-6655-0675-5 (e)

Print information available on the last page.

This book is printed on acid-free paper.

Welcome

This is for you.

For when you can't sleep, think straight, and every crazy emotion in-between.

We all go through pain and sometimes the sun gets through the clouds and gives us a glance at what our lives can truly be. This is a story of my life, every emotion and every memory is connected in these poems. Some of these poems are from 2014 all the way to 2020. This is my diary, this is my life in one page poems.

So- come on this never ending journey with me.

May we both see the end the way we hope.

This story is just as much yours as it is mine.

So read, write, and grow with me.

A colorful world

I look around at the world to see all of its beauty,
But I have trouble seeing the colors.
There are bright yellows, and deep blues.
The shining sun illuminating the oceans below.

I know these colors exist, but I can't seem to find them.
I hear them talk, about how such warm colors make them feel.
The sensation of the most astonishing comfort.
Like a loving hug from the one whom neglects you most.

Extravagant reds, in every heart attached to another.
My heart is on its own, longing for that feeling of comfort the sun gives.
It has been so long since my soul has felt the touch of affection,
It seems that it has lost the ability to feel love.

Everyone wants to feel the warmth of love.
Like that beautiful sun, above the sky.
In these deep waters, I yearn to touch its heat.
I just want to be like all the rest.

Lying in the sun, surrounded by its warmth;
While I'm struggling in the waters I can hardly see.
That sun makes you warmer, while the water makes me colder.
Should I hold my breath or float to the surface.

This colorless ocean turns to a gentle lake; light in color, but it's color.

I can see that cheerful sun laughing to me, reaching out to me.

The water is no longer cold, the world is no longer frigid.

I take one last breath before welcoming the sun into my life, it's light overwhelms me…

Prince of the light

I'm afraid to fall asleep.
I fear losing the memory of you,
Or you losing the memory of me.
Don't forget me, please, even when I am gone.
I don't want to close my eyes because I know tears will fall.
Another lonely night of wondering,
Another lonely night of questioning.
I say I love you, but that's not true.
I could love you, easily, I could.
But I don't yet, but I want to.
I care about you more than anyone else, I look to you for safety.
When I walk into a room, I hope you are there.
You are never there, and when you are, twelve other girls follow behind.
You cared for me, you loved me when no one else did.
Now, all I wish to do is care for you, and make sure you know how much you are loved.
Never forget me my little prince, because if you did, I wouldn't be able to live.
You are my prince of the light.
The light that guides my weary soul to a happy ending that is unknown.

Flowers growing

Your love is like a flower, and your soul is like the stem.
I act like I don't love you, but I can no longer pretend.
It's raining in my mind, it's ruining the flower.
I'm trying to be strong, but you've stolen all my power.
I smile through the pain, and act like I'm okay.
But I'm dying on the inside, it's driving me insane.
The flower begins to wilt, it seems to lose its luster.
I see you moving on, afraid you'll find another.
Your love is like a flower, and you soul is like the stem.
I want to be your other half, but I know that we're just friends.

Waters Raging

I swear as I looked upon the ocean.
The waves crashing in the sea.
The beautiful dangerous commotion,
As the darkness surrounds me.

The sounds of the water falling on to the sand,
It's memorizing, sucking me in.
I'm so lost in the dark sea of life.
It's so frightening, but you can't help but jump in.

Every day is different, ever changing.
Nothing will ever be the same.
I'm staring into the waters raging,
And I'm calling your name.

Skin

Every page of a journal is like a layer of my skin.
You take it for granted, and every layer you peel back causes a deeper pain.
No one notices the wrinkles or scars... the stories that lie behind them.
Who are you to say they aren't important.
But I guess you'd be right.

Dreams

It's like a dream,
A fairy tale never been told before. I could never truly explain how I feel at this moment.
This life, this world, I wish not to wake.
But all dreams come to a close.
At one point or another.
The dreams become nightmares.
I wish for another dream, just one.
Another fairy tale, even if it has been told a thousand times before.

Him

Stop denying it, you're in love with him.

He makes you feel wanted and special.

The sound of his name makes you smile.

He's the one person you always think about but you know you shouldn't.

You're in love with him, you may not want to be, but everyone knows you are.

He may be the only person out there that doesn't know.

But that's a good thing.

You don't want him to know.

Yet you feel like he does.

He could for all you know.

People say he feels the same, but you know that is not the case.

He couldn't be, who would want you.

Who could love a person who is as insignificant as you.

You're nothing special, yet he makes you feel that way.

You're not wanted, yet, for a moment he takes the sadness from your mind and fills it with a tender love not one person can fill.

You're not loved the way you love him.

You'll move on, find someone else to love, someone that won't love you back.

It's nothing new to you, you know how it feels not to be loved.

That's why you'll move on.

But right now, you love him.

You're in love with him.

And that's alright with you.

Don't get lost

Nothing is more troubling when the mind goes blank
It's like the dark of night, the latest of hours.
No moon, and no stars to lead the way.
Feeling so lost in your thoughts
No one else around you.
Nothing to be heard.
Only the steady and hard sound of your breathing.
Like the wind.
Screaming, howling, cold, and dark.
Every gust sounding like your name.
Walking alone, not knowing where to go next.
It's like there's something out to get you.
But there is nothing stronger than you.
Don't get lost in the dark
Because it will not be that way for long.
The light of the night will lift.
And you will walk back home.

Your turn to write

Over

Is this the beginning of the story or are we traveling back in time.

How could any of us tell… we can't.

Not until it's over.

We're all just sitting around waiting for it to be over.

At least I can't wait for it to be over.

Maybe if I just close my eyes for awhile time will go by faster.

And it will finally be over.

Music in My Life

Music surrounds my life like the air I breath. Every moment of each day is filled with music, whether I realize it or not. The power of song is what gives me the passion to do anything in my life. Therefore, it is difficult to pin point a place where it lies. A more challenging question would be where it is not? Music makes me so ecstatic I don't know where to begin. Music comes from happiness, and music comes from pain. Every emotion imaginable, music is the end result. So where do I see music in my life, everywhere. The moment I awaken, the day is a new song. In the silences of my room, the quietness of my thoughts, a tune will find its way through the walls. I can never stay sad when there is music in the world. So, I write songs, despite not being able to write notes, I only need the words. Writing music is easy to me, its poetry. Music is like the air I breath, I couldn't live without it even if I wanted to.

Remember

Remember to believe in yourself, even when it seems like no one else does. Remember to breathe, relax, and always have something to look forward to. Remember to stop half-assing the things you do. If you aren't passionate- stop. Smile when it rains and always bring change around with you. Help those who need it and accept help when it's offered to you. Keep your eyes open, but also you heart. Don't push people away and remember you are loved. Remember these things and you'll always be remembered.

Deep

Deep water and shallow thoughts.
Trying to find what I have lost.
Knowing I'd never discover my wantings, but hoping that someday it would try to find me.
Maybe if I just stopped looking, my needs would come to me.
Maybe if I pushed myself to focus on other things I'd find what I really was looking for.
Shallow water and deep thoughts.
I've come to terms with what I'm not.

Close your eyes and imagine a tall tree- the wind blowing so hard you have to readjust your feet. Slowly look up, all the way to the top and see if you can catch a glimpse of those baby birds being fed in-between the branches. See the mother bird gently care for her children. You have to keep readjusting your feet to keep from falling over. After some time passes you decide to sit and lean up against the tree, give the birds some privacy. Before you know it, your eyes are closed and you're just quietly still, listening to the wind, the birds, the trees. It's like having an out of body experience- being in two places at once. Seeing, doing, being. Which is real and what is next? Readjust your feet and prepare to stand. Use the tree for help- its always going to have your back. Are your eyes open and can you see the deer with her babies? Don't walk any closer- just smile and watch them. Be kind to the world and it will be kind to you. Open you eyes slowly and take a deep breath.

You made it.

Thank

Thank the clouds for the sun they let in.
I thank the atmosphere for protecting me everyday.
I thank the sun for warming me and giving me light when
I open my eyes.

Thank the grass for tickling your feet.
I thank the soil for giving the grass beautiful flowers.
I thank the flowers for bringing a smile to my face without
fail.

Thank the air for giving you life.
I thank the wind for blowing the hair from my face and
making my cheeks pink with the chill.
I thank the sound of leaves rustling and branches brushing
with each movement.

Thank the planet for caring for us even when we don't care
for it.
I thank the planet by cleaning up after myself and others.
I thank the planet by reducing my waste.
I thank the planet by trying my best.

Random Thoughts

~Trying new things can be scary, but continuing to do the same things that harm you is far more frightening.

~When opening up to people, open up in layers... Like each moment allows for another memory.

~Loving someone and them loving you back isn't always enough.

~Time moves slowly when it's waited on, like a women longing for perfection.

~Not everyone will believe you, and that's okay.

~Smile in the dark, your teeth will light the way.(That's Corny)

~As long as you're happy it doesn't matter what you do.

~It isn't hard to love someone when you long to be loved, only when you love yourself does it become more difficult.

Stuck

I'm stuck in the in-between.
Where should I go?
I'm afraid to ask for help, but God knows how badly I need it.
It feels like everyone knows what I'm going through, yet no one offers a hand or a thought.
I'm so tired of feeling alone and doing things on my own.

I'm stuck in the middle ground.
Do I keep my pain to myself, or do I try and get ahead?
It seems that no one is ready to actually listen, just over played inspirational crap rolls off their dry tongues with emptiness behind their eyes.

I'm stuck in hibernation.
Counting down the days until I open my eyes.
There's a chance I wont, but I'm hoping for the best.
I'm wondering if someone is out there watching over me, protecting me.
I'd like to think there is, but I guess we'll never know.

A 3 minute poem

It's almost like I've lost my voice. I yelled and called out and no one was listening. Now no one can listen because my voice is just, gone. I see you walk away from me again and there is nothing left for me to say because I don't even have the words. So, my voice is tried and gone. Nothing left to speak, nothing left to hear.

It's almost like I've lost my sight. My glasses are broken and my vision is all distorted. You kept leaving me again, so the light never bothered to return. I'm looking all around me, but there is nothing left to see, there is nothing here to see me.

It's almost like I've died. I'm a ghost walking around all alone because you left me again. You say I can't move on or make a new friend- but you aren't even a friend to me. I've done nothing but try and save you. When you were the one hurting yourself. There is nothing left for me to do and there is nothing you can do that will help me forgive.

Sing with me.

I am a broken record, cracked and damaged.
Damaged by those who played me.
They flip me over and act like they don't use me- but they do.
Am I drawn to pain?
It seems like it's all I really want.
The same songs continue to play on my heart.
I'm screaming, but to them I'm just standing in silence.
I'm trying too hard to find happiness, I'll never find it.
But I'll never stop trying.
I like the pain too much, it's all I've ever known.

Let's play a game

The pain is written in my heart, but I wish it could be written on my skin.

If you could see what goes through my mind, would you look at me the same way?

I want the world to know how much hurt I feel, but they could never know, it's not in the cards.

It took me years to accept myself, and truly let people see me, but they still don't see all of me.

The pain in my soul is too much to carry, I need to cut it out.

I am strong, I will not look away from God's light, but why is it that I have to feel like this.

How are you feeling?

There's something about you.

You make even my most fearful insecurities seem minimal. The things I hate about myself, you show them love; and that reminds me that I should love them.

No matter who said I was ugly, no matter what my mind tells me. You show me that I am beautiful.

Your gentle touch calms my storms, it brings the sunshine back to the day light, I couldn't imagine life without you.

You have taught me to love, truly love. It has been such a short time, but I feel like I've known you my whole existence. Thank you for being perfect to me and reminding me that I am perfect the way I am.

Spirit

Sometimes I wonder what it would be like to walk the earth as a spirit. Almost like I was never here at all. To wear a Cloak that hides my limbs and hides my memories.

Sometimes I wonder what is thought of me, good or bad, or maybe nothing at all. If my existence is noticed or if my breath is just something that is part of someone else' after thought.

Sometimes I wonder if I'd be missed or cried for. Will it matter to man if one less bed was taken, if one less check was written, if one less was here?

What if I was a spirit walking the soil like a worm. What if my Cloak took all memory away and there was nothing left but some ownerless memories.

Tired

How truly tiring it is to feel every emotion everyday. To feel a sense of calm and hope for you future when you wake. To accept you present life for what it is, yet not fully understanding where it could take you. Feeling trapped and lazy, thinking you're not doing enough or that you just aren't enough. As the day flashes onward it can feel like months are flying by...

I'm so tired.

I feel lost and sad and there isn't anything I can do at this point but feel angry. I feel so angry and let down. Yet, it's because of my own choices- all that I regret. Some things I can't really change, but there's a part of me that wishes I could have overcome those choices.

No matter how small.

You believe me, right?

I remember when I told you. We were in the car.

I didn't want to tell you, but someone found out and said I had to tell you.

I hid my dirty secret for over a decade, but I told the wrong person.

I didn't want to tell you. But I did.

You believed me, you actually did.

You said you knew something happened that day, but you didn't know what.

You believed me.

You asked if I wanted to talk about it, if I wanted therapy, or anything. But I wasn't ready, I had to act like it didn't matter- or I wouldn't have survived.

All I wanted was for you to stop talking to me about your friends, I asked you to leave me out of the trips and phone calls, but you didn't.

You picked your friendships with them over me and my pain.

I was in the fourth grade and I've hated myself ever since.

You believed me, but you didn't care enough to remember.

You are loved, write about it

Fire

Secrets spread like wild fire. All it takes is one match to burn down the whole forest. Even when you extinguish the flames the evidence is still apparent on the bark of the trees. The fight could be between the flames and a tree, but eventually everything is involved and everything dies.

We leave this earth alone.

The stress of life cripples the soul, yearning for that full feeling again. You try to move on but something about it keeps sucking you in. The misconstrued intoxication of hate builds in your mind. No one understands that feeling alone is an emotion you never get used to. It's something you just have to live with.

Window

Looking out an old and withered window, tattered and worn from a long life lived. It may be weak and cold to the touch, but it holds up and stays strong. For the house, and those who live in it, the window stays strong.

Windows are a gate way for change, they can expose so much or as little as they wish. That is all you need, a window of opportunity. A window to break in order to set a path for others. A window to hide behind, or a window too open to set one free.

Windows can provide safety and warmth, or air and free will. Windows are all you need. I am day dreaming, people watching, writing, and hoping. These windows are teaching me to cope.

I am protected by these windows. The thick and tall, new, clean, and clear windows. The withered and beaten, old, faded, and dusty windows. Each window has meaning and every view has a memory; more to be forgotten and all to be discovered.

I am a window, look within me and explore my pains.

Keep pushing.

Such kind eyes; a willow tree smiles my way.
Giving me such hope; the start of a new day.
Moving on and starting over; No more wishing on that four leaf clover.
Throw away the old and welcome the fresh, putting these new hopes to the test.
I see a new day, with a smile on my face.
Push the past out of the way, pick up the pace.

Self-Worth

The self worth felt from within, it is not an external force that changes us; self worth in controlled by us. Looking in the old window, the reflection of a person valuable to whomever is near us. I stand there, looking deeply at my flaws, the things I once loved, now ugly.

My hair, the color seemingly shiny in the rays of the sun. The way it parts, I never really noticed it before. After a few moments I realized I was lost in my own eyes. Observing and analyzing each color and shade, uniquely mine. I broke away; my nose, my cheek bones, my forehead. Each and every characteristic, mine.

I hated them, I was disgusted by the way God made me. If He loved me so much how could He make me like this. I took a step back to see all of me. My arms, legs, hands, and fingers. I stare at my finger nails with ware and faded life, is this how people see me. With ware and faded life.

I feel my heart ache with longing. I hurt and I hate, I wish and I love. I want to love myself.

My self worth is non-existent because I allow others to control my life. Will I be able to love these ears, my stomach, and my heart. My self worth is controlled by me, not by those around me. I must take control of my own life, because if I cannot take care of myself- who will?

There is always a secret peaking between the curtains.

Part of me is hurting,
but part of me is not.
The external part is smiling,
Yet the internal part has stopped.
I am not broken and I am not torn;
However, my edges may be a bit worn.
They've crumbled the paper,
and set it a flame.
They want it to flatten,
But I will never be the same.

Left out to dry, but all that was wet was my eyes.

Abandoned-
By those who you loved most.
By those who hurt you more.
Left alone-
Unloved and hungry,
For the birds to feed upon.
Why are good people the most broken down.
Build me up-
Alone I overcome what destroyed me.
My foundation will be stronger.
Built with love for loving.
I will not abandon my home.

Let me run away.

Even in the most crowded spaces I can feel isolated. When the conversations are louder than my thoughts all I can do is put my headphones in and close my eyes. The noise helps the silence needed to survive. The larger the party, the more intimate, but all the more reason to feel lonely.

Maybe you should forget me.

When the darkness over shadows even the heaviest clouds we forget there was ever light. When the light is missing from our view for too long, we mistake those clouds for sunshine. When will the light remind me that darkness is only part of the journey.

Express and rant

I don't think I ever said goodbye.

Hi.
It's been awhile.
I've been thinking about you lately.
I guess a lot, recently.
There's an endless amount of non-existent memories in my mind.
Many thoughts of 'if she came', but you didn't.
And it's not your fault.

I've been thinking about the family recently.
How it's broken and distant.
How screams of hate over the phone mask the pain everyone feels.
The endless amount of 'they can't come over',
The dozens of 'the plans have changed'.
I wish things could have been better for you.

It's been awhile.
I think about you pretty much everyday.
I wish you could have been here longer.
Maybe the family would have been happier,
I know I would have been.
Just know I love you.

I know they're hurting and no one can express it.
I just wish things were different.
I wish that the hate turned to compassion and the pain turned to love.

I'd like to think you'd like that.
I'd like to think that if you were still here everyone would be happy.
But I don't think they were ever happy.

I've been thinking about you a bunch these days.
I hope I cross your mind every once in awhile.
Bye.

Something with me.

Something in the wind, or the air.
Someone whispering my name, or so I think.
Do I hear sirens or is it my ears trying to fill in the silence.
I'd call out to the emptiness in hopes of an answer, but no
sounds comes out.
Instead I stand there, silent still, eyes wide.
It has to be something in the wind, or the air.
Someone was here, but they're gone now.
It's just me standing in the silence of the brush.
Tall trees and small shrubbery.
I hear no rustling, the silence is too loud.
The sirens of passed emergency, the energy of a memory.
It might have been the wind, or the air.
I think it was me whispering my name, or so I think.
I've been standing here alone for far too long.
I forget what the sound of sirens feels like.
Or how to get home.

That's what you think

Your truths are so compelling it's almost like they're lies.

Your words are so powerful it's like you're hiding behind them.

The judgment in your eyes is like a wall of knives coming closer and closer, until I can no longer stand the pain you cause.

Let me leave you alone- let me finally do something for myself.

Your lies are so deceitful, it's almost like you're being honest.

Don't forget me when I'm gone.

I am writing my needs out in blood but the rain keeps washing them away.

Sitting in a puddle that is slowly growing deeper still.

Every painful memory turns to words on my skin.

Each cut deeper than the last.

Every scar wanting to tell its story.

I want to see the world from a perspective that is not my own.

I am not my own.

Sometimes I like to dream inside my mind.
I wonder what it's like on the outside.
To see myself as someone else,
If they see me like I do.
Is it even possible to be the main character in your own story.
What is it like on the surface, where the pain is not my own.
To be someone else's story.

I'm always Afraid.

Should I be brave or should I hide away.
I make people leave because I'm afraid they won't stay.
I'm told my feelings matter but I'm not allowed to say a word- why does it seem like nothing I say is ever heard.
From across the room you can hear my laugh, but in my heart are steal traps.
Everything goes in but nothing comes out, so all I do is hurt to save myself from what I'm afraid of.

Not everything makes sense.

I may regret this, but it has to be said.
I may wish I didn't, but if I don't, I'll wish I did.
All stories deserve to be told and heard, so here we are.

I was told once that art isn't art unless it's shared with the world.
I still don't know if that's true, but if it is...
I guess this will be the final experiment.

I was told once that lying was a form on expression.
To go on the stage of life and sell my soul to the capitalist king.
I don't know if that's true, but in case it is...
I guess this will be the final experiment.

I was told once that being scared was a strength.
That I should be afraid of my choices so I made the best ones I could.
I don't know if that's true, but by change that it is...
I guess this will be the final experiment.

I may regret this, but it needed to be said.
Since I did, I may have wished I didn't.
All stories deserve to be told and heard, so here we are.

Write it out, don't forget to date it!

Don't worry about me.

I want to be buried in a pretty coffin next to an empty plot for the husband I never had. I have some drawings of different flowers you could use as a stencil. Just, please be kinder to the land I lay underneath than you were to me when I sat above it.

I ask very little of you, but if you could- do one last thing. I want the viewing to be on a weekend so all My friends can come. Let anyone that has the words- to speak. Even if that means there is no words at all. I want to hear them tell me they love me... all the way from heaven.

Take pictures of my friends and family with a Polaroid camera and put them in my chipped finger painted hands, so I have them with me always. Close all the blinds and light a candle for each year I walked the earth, but leave a window open in the back so I can see. Say what you hated along with what you loved, I want everyone to be honest for once. I want to hear the reasons I left this place and if anyone even knows why.

I wish you'd all just open your ears and hear me. Why aren't you listening to me. Why am I screaming at the top of my lunges for someone to see behind my eyes when no one is even willing to open their own. I have no more voice left- I've given it all away. ..To people who didn't care to see it's worth.

Just remember: I didn't lose a battle I fought hard to win. I finished a battle I was ready to let go.

The Mentor.

Sometimes you don't realize how lucky you are until you were.

I was lucky to have someone in my life who believed in me like a father. Who spoke to me like a partner and protected me like a brother.

I had a mentor in my life that wanted me and my ambitions, not the attention my ambitions brought him. He used my weaknesses as strengths to make me strong. He didn't use my strengths to become all I was.

The mentor I needed was one who let me talk when I had questions and walked me through my fog. Not one that talked through his life and used unknown experiences as lessons.

I didn't realize how lucky I was until I didn't have that anymore. But if he can move on to bigger things-
So can I.

Thank you for everything

CPSIA information can be obtained
at www.ICGtesting.com
Printed in the USA
BVHW030203020621
608622BV00012B/73